all the time more than anything

poems by

Emily Zogbi

Finishing Line Press
Georgetown, Kentucky

all the time more than anything

poems

Copyright © 2023 by Emily Zogbi
ISBN 979-8-88838-388-9 First Edition
All rights reserved under International and Pan-American Copyright Conventions. No part of this book may be reproduced in any manner whatsoever without written permission from the publisher, except in the case of brief quotations embodied in critical articles and reviews.

Publisher: Leah Huete de Maines
Editor: Christen Kincaid
Cover Art and Design: Victoria D'Esposito
Author Photo: Pete Perry

Order online: www.finishinglinepress.com
also available on amazon.com

Author inquiries and mail orders:
Finishing Line Press
P. O. Box 1626
Georgetown, Kentucky 40324
U. S. A.

Table of Contents

I.

IN THE GLASSHOUSE 1
FABLE 2
THE WORLD (REVERSED) 3
KINGS PARK PSYCHIATRIC CENTER 4
THE TOWER 6
BAREFOOT IN THE KITCHEN, MY MOTHER TELLS ME
   ABOUT THE DREAM 7
HYPERGRAPHIA 8
SAINT LUCY MAKES A RUN FOR IT 9
AT THE HOSPITAL 10
ODE TO CRAZY GIRLS 12
GROCERY DREAM 14
WORDS UNDERLINED IN A USED COPY OF THE
   COLLECTED POEMS OF SYLVIA PLATH 16
I HELP LARA CROFT WITH HER FIRST KILL 17
BEFORE BEING FOUND 18
THE MIDWIFE 19
PUTTING ON EMILY DICKINSON'S CLOTHES 20
WORD PLAY 22
PAST / PRESENT / FUTURE 23
THE GOOD DOG 24
LOST THINGS 25
CRYING AT SUNSETS 26

II.

SATURDAY 33
GHOST STORY 34
THE GREAT FORGETTING 35
MARY ANSWERS ALL MY QUESTIONS 37
GRIEF 38
NESTING 39

HOME FOR DINNER 40
HOME FOR DINNER, REPRISE 41
THE ARCHETYPE 42
ANNA M. 43
BAD LUCK POEM 45
ADAM FORCING EVE TO EAT AN APPLE 46
DREAM CATACLYSM OR TERMINATOR 2 IS THE
   BETTER MOVIE 47
SUNDOWN 48
THE NEIGHBOR 50
MYTH MAKER 51
THIS DAY 52
PAST / PRESENT / FUTURE 53
THINGS WE DO & HAVE ALWAYS DONE 54

III.
BIRTH OF VENUS 63
DURING A CHAT SESSION, THE THERAPIST
   DISCOURAGES ME FROM ASTRAL PROJECTION 64
A GUIDE FOR MOVING THROUGH 66
MYTHOLOGY 68
HEAVY 70
I FEEL LIKE A GIRL... 72
ODE TO A HOME WAXING KIT 73
AT THE HOSPITAL, AGAIN 74
CHERYL CRANE REMEMBERS THE FLOWERS 76
ME & MOM & LITTLE GIRL BLUE 77
PAST / PRESENT / FUTURE 78
I STAND GRIPPING THE BRIDGE 79
VIGNETTES FROM THE END 80
ODE TO A SCENE IN MOONSTRUCK 83
WHEN THE STORY ENDS 84

for my family, more than anything

I.

O holy figure at the edge of my bed
He leaned in closely and said nothing to me
Repeating image of you when I'm alone
I see you calling to me, then I see nothing at all

Now, Now

IN THE GLASSHOUSE

Susanne Ussing, 1980, ceramic and photography, 10x10x10m

Mom said she dreamt of little girls
while I was just a guppy
nestled in the crook of her pelvis,
curled in on myself, shy
from before I was even a real thing,
not ready for the world
to know me yet. She never
dreamed I'd become this
massive; ghost, guttural
scream at the foot of her bed,
depression floating like a dead fish
in my gut. Woman in the glass
house grows to fill the space
she's put in, is made of paper
and bones and spitfire.
Born to be contained, held
together with iron and glue.
The artist (her mother)
adds another layer. She grows.
She is kneeling, always,
even in art she must be naked, crouched,
miniature, Lady Homunculus.
Here, in the glass jar, distilled
air, thick with vanilla,
she becomes herself.

FABLE

Mother Goose and her husband's ghost
lean into the kitchen radio, sway
to the tune of baseball. The children come
with Kents and lotto tickets. She accepts
their change in quarters, taps a seed of ashes
out the open window. *Why's it so loud?*
they ask, palming cigarettes between each other
while she cleans the oven. The ghost erupts
in laughter. *Just so he can listen*, she replies.
There is, apparently, no baseball where ghosts live.

Outside an eggplant tree sprouts upward.
Heavy purple, big as moons, she slices them
thin, fries them in a pan and the children
pick them from the oil, chew the browned edges,
lick their fingers clean.

THE WORLD (REVERSED)

I used to have a yellow parakeet called Happy
who'd throw himself against the door of his cage.
He vanished one day out an open window.
I can't say I particularly care
about the names of certain animals,
what they eat or what eats them,

but today I saw three dragonflies resting
on the felled tree next to the riverbank.
What weird birds those are. I assumed
it must be luck to see three at once.
One had the face of a lion and the hands of a person
I loved whose voice was not a voice

I recognized. A deer
that was not a deer but was maybe
a tree came forward, gracefully
disjointed, and looked right at me. A friend said
she touched it and it spoke to her. I laid my hand
flat and wide on its trunk. It said nothing

and I was afraid. I heard about her car, the way it soared
into the median and she herself began to fly
before landing with a soft crack
in the overgrowth, her wingspan stretched from here

to here.

KINGS PARK PSYCHIATRIC CENTER

The giant is turning to dust
in the next town over. Teenagers drive past
her hunched corpse in the dark,

crawl inside her stomach to smoke
and dare each other to climb 13 stories
into her mouth, hunt for whatever

ghosts are left, the bones
she's picked her teeth with.
All tombs are abandoned

eventually. A baseball game screams to life
in a field nearby. A man walks his dog.
Children ride their bikes.

The Sound folds itself against the bluffs.
This is public property
and she has always been here.

Katelyn kicks a soda can
across faded graffiti and it skitters
like a spider into a pile of glass.

She's like, *It's weird to think,*
back in the '50s or whatever,
we probably would've been here.

We tilt our heads back, strain
to see her mayhemed face
in all those vines,

the ice picks
and pillowcases,
a hole in every ancient fence.

In death, a giant's body
becomes another hill
for us to sprint down.

How many of me lie inside her,
harpooned into submission,
whale skeleton, full of paper.

THE TOWER

My family has a habit of seeing flickers in the dark. The night her mother died my grandma saw a silent figure at the foot of her bed. The children recall women in white. Clouds in the living room. I am watching my father watch his father become a shadow. There is the hall light, his weeping silhouette.

> some cancers make
> our fathers small
> as baby teeth

Last I saw of my grandfather, he was charging into a Christmas night. I'm trying to think of a new metaphor for death. Like a carton of eggs jumping from the countertop: yolk shell membrane splattered across the kitchen floor.

> breakfast is over
> and we mourn the clean plate
> it could have lived on

My father and I take the long drive upstate and come upon a rock formation. *When I was thirteen, I hid a penny here*, he says. I run my hand along a shelf above my head, kick up dust and spiders. The penny appears in my palm.

> a quivering hand
> can no longer note
> the cardinal in the window

There is the person you were before and the person you are after—you flipped around. Negative of yourself navigating a world in reflections. He remembers a hiding place, a cabin in the woods. Now, it is only a painting above the bed, but once belonged to summers of copper pennies and eggs, fresh as orange suns.

> he sees a ghost
> and knows a tower
> has crumbled

BAREFOOT IN THE KITCHEN, MY MOTHER TELLS ME ABOUT THE DREAM

It's been happening a lot. I couldn't see his feet.
I can't remember what kind of shoes he wore.
It's driving me crazy.

I'm a kid. It's me and him and all my sisters.
We're playing, chasing each other. There's a door
and we run through it.

He won't follow. I look at him. *Aren't you coming?*
He smiles and shrugs. *There's nothing I can do*
or *There's nowhere I can go.*

Do you remember when he died. You were so young.
Turns out, when a milk truck crashes,
there is rarely a spill.

You only met him the one time. Do you remember
the funeral. It never made sense to me
—a grave without a headstone. A hole without a body.

Anyway, we're going to your grandmother's house.
The bird died. His corpse is in the freezer.
She wants him buried in the sun.

HYPERGRAPHIA

> *Emma Hauck was involuntarily committed to a psychiatric hospital in 1909. She wrote letters to her husband in frantic, overlapping text. They bore the repeating phrase: "Sweetheart, come." None were sent.*

Here, in the attic, I wait for you.
I worry about the milk
spilled like fog across the morning,
the jackals that came to lap at it.
I couldn't do anything but scream
when I saw them, their yellow moons.
I know I am just a memory now.
My incurable symptom. Sweet,
I am walking on air. You don't have to know
what became of me to see it.
The women came
to look, mouths open
like jewelry boxes freshly rummaged.
They see themselves in graphite,
the ridge of their left hand sore with
loss, howling
for the forgiveness of paper.
                              Collect me, heart.
I am but a stone in your breast
I am only a pocket.
I want the countryside. Cake.
I want to dance.

Maybe your kiss was a kind of mercy—
those lips that vanished me.
Forgiving sun, long morrow.
Here, in the attic, I wait for you.

      come, come, come

SAINT LUCY MAKES A RUN FOR IT

Where do you think you're going
with your plastic shopping bags
full of nightgowns and jewelry
dumped from your dresser
like oysters from a net.

You cannot take it with you, you say
to the shadow who lurks in the corner,
black blood pouring from his mouth,
eyes served on a silver plate.

He tried to move you once,
in a dream, burn you into crumbs.
When the flame would not catch,
hitched you to a team of oxen.
When you would not break,
shoved a sword through your neck.

The hospital is not a hospital
and you know it. Black smoke pours
like oysters from your throat. The shadow says,
If you run, they cannot catch you.

You wake to him and cannot scream.
Your mother's rings, the nightgowns,
the plastic shopping bags—you wake to him
and cannot scream. You are lucid and righteous.
He left you, he guides you, muttering, fumbling

in the cold for forgotten keys.

AT THE HOSPITAL

How is it remember

the red gash crown grinning

the red sound of the ghost

in the corner.

if everything's alright

to eat, good to slice,

of children bathed in sun

I didn't hear

on the phone, but woke

its ringing filled the house.

in our beds to reach

My mother grabs my hand.

very good at this,

cry. She catches

like the arm of a running child.

one more time

before we go, let me just

Ma. Is everything alright

now, before the doors close.

the red house,

across her forehead,

chewing watermelon rinds

Three soft knocks to check

inside. It's good

to serve the mouths

and nothing else.

you cry

seconds before

At once we shifted

for the cradle.

I'm not gonna be

she says, but doesn't

the elevator door

Let me make sure

that she's asleep,

—Have you eaten,

in there. Do you need me

trail of black seeds

toward the window.

Before the room reddens,

crawling

ODE TO CRAZY GIRLS

        Ah, to be a skeleton in a woman-suit
awash in the scream of trumpets. It matters less
who writes the song when they all sound the same.
        The end is here
and the end is a good friend of mine
who hangs around after everyone
leaves the party. We shotgun
something sweet in my bathtub,
crush the cans against our heads
and gossip about the abandoned
buildings on the edge of town
        and the parking lots
where I'd tilt my head and lean,
arms folded, against a lover's car.
I don't need fire or lighter fluid
to burn my instrument
just two hands and the will to do so.
        As a child, I found a robin's egg
and, thinking it a forgotten Easter decoration,
smashed it against a tree. I'm sure
there was a lesson in the rivulets of yolk
that ran down my arm while I cried
for my mother. When I want to break something
        I should.
There is no sugar in this house, just a girl
who bloomed into a broken dish, knelt
on kitchen tile and plucked each piece by hand,
considered the wild lines I could draw
with a mosaic. The end
        is here—2:37 A.M. on a Tuesday:
refrigerator door swinging open
like the flag of a surrendering army.
Light bleeds out onto my bare thighs
while I eat grape jelly with a spoon.
        Every episode begins
on the kitchen floor; in the bedroom
in the dark; in the bathroom

with the shower on; heaving over a toilet bowl
until what comes up is my mother's voice
on the other end of the phone.
I drink until I am full
        and never stop,
not until the entire house
is empty, all the sugar melted
at the bottom of my glass.

GROCERY DREAM

An urgency to explain
I dreamt of you

or the back of your head
and the backs of lots of heads

I know. You saw me
over your shoulder

but didn't stop so
I followed and lost you

in the produce section.
I could've held you

in my hand, turned you about
to look for spots.

Where do I appear
in heads I know

and heads I don't?
He dreamt of my mother

before they met, saw
the back of her head

on the sidewalk.
She had no feet.

He couldn't catch her.
Have you seen me

before, in the bread aisle
perhaps? Am I with you

by the apples?
Am I like my mother

in dreams? I have her feet.
Am I uncatchable? Do I

take something green and bite
deep, half-mooned?

WORDS UNDERLINED IN A USED COPY OF THE COLLECTED POEMS OF SYLVIA PLATH

These halls are full of women who think they are birds.
Involved in its weird blue dreams,
Stars hung water-sunk,
What did they know that I didn't?
the authentic sea denies them and will pluck
Their veins as white as porkfat.
fantastic flesh down to the honest bone.
Litter the mud like orangepeel.
This pair seek single state from that dual battle.
Soft suede tongues between his bones.
That wrestle us like angels;
Slowly she spins the ball: O the beauty of usage!
Knifelike, he was chaste enough.
And his blood beating the old tattoo
That truant heart
If only the wind would leave my lungs alone.
I must make more maps.
The sun's corrosive wintering— Arrowy ray
The baby carp Looks up.
Sun-moneyed God-fathered
lean to my wound; burn on, burn on
I am, I am, I am. Pure death's-metal.
It would take more than a lightning-stroke
the weedy acres of your brow
Into my most chaste own eyes
To create such a ruin.
The day forgets itself.
I am all mouth.

I HELP LARA CROFT WITH HER FIRST KILL

in high definition / I can watch her / get mauled by
a bear / a mountain lion / a man / impaled on
a loose piece of metal / a tree branch / a spike
protruding from the ground / drowned in
a river / the ocean / a shallow puddle
of mud / it doesn't matter how
\/
it happens / every time / she
screams / moans / grunts / gasps / she
makes it fun / makes me want
to hear the squelch / as she's sliced apart by
an airplane propeller / a boat propeller
a chopper's static wing
\/
I've spent a lot of time / with her / Me + Lara
build a fire / Me + Lara
learn to / see in the dark / be invisible / weep
in private / light a funeral pyre / Me + Lara
learn to / be an animal / go into caves
full of / wolves / come back
\/
changed / ravenous / when he / grabs us / his hand
slithers up our / arm / engulfs our / chin / we know
to / reel back / go for the eyes + / dig / gnash +
grab / anything solid / smash / smash / smash / not stop
till his skull is / a shattered teapot / Lara
retches / turns to the sky / cries
\/
oh god as in / there is no turning back
oh god as in / I had no choice
oh god as in / this was going to happen anyway
\/
in the beginning / Lara is / trapped / crawling
towards / daylight / she's dirty
+ broken / + bursts
through the earth / I think
she's not gonna make it / then
she does

BEFORE BEING FOUND

Green feet glide
downward around
rocks, branches, weeds,
the glittering liquid light
above me, unsettling
and familiar. The sky
collapses into puddles
and sends the children
running. I'm not lost.
I'm mud. I see no rain
      from here, no
thing wrapped in plastic,
no lines, no pink fish
or beautiful balloons floating
out the windows of rooms
I love, or children's teeth
kept safe in a teakettle.
On a night like this the boys
should've wrapped their car
neatly around a tree.
I like to be quick.
I like to leave early
before something large
and strange is hoisted
from the river. Tell me,
are you a holy swan?

THE MIDWIFE

What will they do with me next?
　　　　　　—animatronic witch, Salem Witch Museum

　　　History lies
in the bodies of children
who entered the world
through her open hands
　　　It's the Devil's work
to protect the fortress
of a mother's body
as it expels the shrieking
mouth of a new life
　　　Evergreen image
suspended forever in flight
　　　I saw her dance
barefoot against the earth
She'll be thrown to the lake
with stones in her mouth
There are several ways
to unmake a body
　　　A legacy of ash
Fear snapped
from her neck
like a string of pearls

PUTTING ON EMILY DICKINSON'S CLOTHES

after sam sax and Billy Collins

She interrupts herself—
makes her body small enough
to fit on the back of an envelope.

I pass her the bone-ribbed corset
first, pull the strings until
she stretches like a shadow.

Limp hands rest in a naked lap.
Hair hangs around her face,
shoulders curve in.

I'll tell this story sideways until scraps
sprout into full sheets of paper and a night
table becomes a grand mahogany desk.

We'd leave the homestead back in Amherst
where it's always quiet, where the ground swells
and Death walks leisurely down the road.

We solve the puzzle of the hook and Eye,
the clasps, the whalebone stays
closed tight around her breast.

I'd like to see her at the ocean,
hard wooden shoes
dangling from her fingertips,

skirt bunched in her fist,
black hair flying in a halo
around her head.

I can show her where I
walked from his house
to the weeping tree,

the tearful march back,
the choicelessness of it all—
an open field in August heat.

In Amherst, I take her dress
off the chair. She knows how it hurts
to live. She wants her clothes back.

I don't notice she's crying
until the dress falls heavy
over her head. Long and white,

the hem landing at her feet
like a sack of flour. I say
nothing.

Last, the hairpins gathered
from the hardwood like shells.
I pull her hair back—

thick curtains drawn to look
at all that rain, the puddles
forming in the orchard.

WORD PLAY

I dug myself up. Long-buried, I keep
her in a cement block in the yard
        along with a book of mix CDs and an old t-shirt.

        She remembers what being-in-love is like.
I think I made her up. I break her out and dance her around.
Anthropometrically identical, she is a desert animal
who writes about love like it's a canyon: to be crossed
        in giant, bounding leaps. She remembers things

        like laughing at the right time.
She's appeared before. You remember. Knee deep
in the mud of our analogy, she called you to me—
a strange chorus that translated to something like:

        Hello sir, is there a portico I can drag you under
        where we may join mouths and hands in the rain
        to sprout a thousand cress weeds,
        white-topped and shining, a field of ash after conflagration,
        while someone inside waits for me under a yellow lamp
        and the light spilling from the windows
        turns the puddles gold?

        Once, some drunk friends and I squatted
against a neighbor's hedge, a steady stream
swirling into the shape of a heart on the sidewalk
        which made perfect sense.

        On a recent Wednesday I paused
at an almost-dried patch of concrete.
Underneath a sneaker print
        and next to a penis

        I carved my initials with the tip of my finger,
then mined gray pebbles from under that nail for days.

        I'd like to be heart-shaped too.

PAST / PRESENT / FUTURE

      I. The Five of Cups

There are not enough hours in the day
for lying around, staring at slats
of light on the bedroom floor,
sighing on the toilet,
manifesting desire in every form.

      I've counted the days in coffee mugs
      grown cold in the afternoon.

      II. The Empress

When I glance at the sink full of dishes, my mother calls.
I turn on the water and roll up my sleeves.

      III. Page of Wands (Reversed)

I, too, would appreciate a very big stick
with which to ward off friends and loved ones.
I, too, have imagined myself upside down
and breathing.

THE GOOD DOG

The dog is dying. Quality of life determined
by whether she can drown in the water dish.
The girl's mother is good at keeping things alive
and some dogs continue to live

when they shouldn't.
One day we'll all be found dead
under a kitchen table. Going home
just makes the girl sad, all those ghosts

dragging themselves across the tile
for one more drink of water, the quiet
frenzy to keep the things we love with us,
nothing tying them here but a prayer card

tucked in the mirror, a red bandana,
a mound of dirt.

LOST THINGS

She gingerly adjusts the statue of Jesus playing football, a stuffed jackalope, a model of Apollo 11. A portrait of her grandfather rests against the wall. His name is on the moon, you know. We collect the Christmas dishes and haul them upstairs. This house is fit to burst. *What a lonely cloud I am* she thinks. Her children plead—there are too many things here. Too many stairs, dollhouses, and piles of ash. Everyone recalls the smell of the electrical fire, rabbit and cat huddled under the kitchen table. Okay everyone, let's play Find the Percocet. Saint Anthony laughs at the top of the stairs. It's always a game with him. I turn over a vase and find my name. I round a corner and the table has vanished. I shake a teapot and the missing rings appear in my mouth. Where'd you find this. Someone is weeping by the mailbox. I am cleaning in a manic frenzy and now the keys are gone. We've all misplaced the boiling water. It's melting the polyester in an eldest daughter's shirt. I forget how to peel a tomato. I forget how to clean chicken. I don't know when I turned the oven on. Who is that man in the portrait. What's that smell. What do you mean he's dead. Do you see that cardinal in the window. Do you see the cloud in the den. I think I know its name. There's a hole in the fence. You wished yourself to the moon and that's where you slipped through.

CRYING AT SUNSETS

I hate the word *tender* and the narcissists who use it
        to describe themselves. Tender once said,
        If I die, you won't be able to mourn me.
        So, I accused Tender of collecting people
              and they went silent for the winter.

Someone who has been dead for a while
        told me I should only write love poems
              when I'm not in love.
        Most of the time I am too annoyed
        to write love poems.
I am not a tender person,
        but I have narcissistic tendencies
        and cry all the time.
When I cry, I stare at myself in the mirror.
        The mirror used to face my bed.
I moved it because an article I skimmed said
        it's bad feng shui and doing this would help me
              sleep. I woke up five times last night
        and stared at the ceiling fan which exists
in a perpetual state of motion.

              Tender once asked, *You weren't waiting for me*
              were you? I didn't ask you to do that
        and I wept an entire February.
        Tender never asked me to do anything
        I wasn't already running towards.

        I have mastered public weeping.
        I am not afraid to cry in front of strangers,
              the same way I'm not afraid
to use public restrooms. Being proud of this
        might make me a narcissist.
Once, on the M train, a puddle of snot
        formed in the scarf covering my face
              and I felt like a coward.

If you live inside of a word,
        cut a clean slit in its belly
and rest in the warm pocket,
        you do not become it.

My obsession with death is hereditary.
    I keep prayer cards tucked in my mirror.
    Mom does this too.
    I carry one of those prayer cards in my wallet
    in case I need to become hysterical on-the-go.
My family sits at the kitchen table and plans funerals.
                Dad wants to be buried
                but mom wants to be cremated
                and have her ashes spread on Robert Moses Beach.
    This makes dad upset.
            I suggest they both do that thing
            where their remains become a tree,
                but I heard about someone's grandfather
                who was planted in the yard:
                he grew over the neighbor's fence
                and started to rot. Eventually
                he had to be thrown
                in a woodchipper.
    I didn't cry at my grandfather's funeral.
        Instead, I avoided the body and hoarded
        brochures about the grieving process.
Yes, *What about cremation?* indeed.
   As many choices as there are wishes.
   For your family's sake.
   Resolving Your Complicated Grief.
   Call Ron today!
            I wanted to give him a dollar
        but when I finally approached the casket
the front pocket of his suit was full.
This is the second time I've seen my father sob. I have an absurd thought
            that if my grandfather had a daughter,
                he would've beaten his sons less.
My grandmother has asked me
    several times to make sure

they never take her back to the hospital.
        She knows she'll die there. I tell her
to use her cane. She's fallen twice
            in the last year. I never call her.
                    Maybe I should talk to Ron.

        There's a man in my family who's been dead
for a while. He'd carve benign tumors from his scalp
            with a pocketknife. Sitting on his front porch
            like he was snapping peas, an ashtray
                  for his cigarettes and a bowl for his disease.
                  He'd soothe the tender wounds by beating his children.

        I often write eulogies in my head
        for people who are still alive
        and end up staring at the mirror too long.
        I like reading people's diaries
        and making wild accusations.
                  My friend hates crying
                    because it makes her look weak.
            I tell her crying is the body's natural response
              to an influx of emotions—they need to get out
somehow. People who don't cry are boring,
but I don't understand people who cry at sunsets.
                I'm jealous of those who know how to hold it.
                    Some skies are just inappropriate.
Recently, I had a dream
      that my brother died. In the dream,
           he'd been dead for a while
                and I was living in that feeling
                      that only happens when someone has been dead
for a while and you forget they've been dead
for a while and want to tell them something
                but remember you can't because they're dead.
            When I woke up, I called him
            because that would be a terrible way
            to find out I'm psychic.

This morning I cried because no one loves me.

This is not an original idea.
    I took one of each brochure
and I'm reaching out to Ron.

II.

All the while, many people are on a bus, drained. Everyone misses someone or is considered missing.

Selah Saterstrom

SATURDAY

for PU, 1957-2019

When, during a fall, do you realize
you're going to break your neck?

Is your mind elsewhere: the snag
in the carpet, who you'll scold

about shoes in the hallway, the betrayal
of gravity as you rush

for the phone? The tulips are large and strange
like they were last summer.

The day passed and I didn't notice. I was obsessing
over what you drank the last time we saw each other.

You were right about growing up
near the ocean. Landlocked here,

I miss large bodies of water more than my family.
I've always liked what I couldn't see

the bottom of and tended towards things
I couldn't prove—but, back to the fall.

You walk into the kitchen. Something big
circles the yard, sniffing for rabbits.

An old-fashioned, straight-backed wooden chair.
A list on the counter but no children to call.

A girl in New York has a bad feeling.
Tomorrow is Sunday, and then what?

GHOST STORY

The cloud in the vestibule does not
look like her uncle who, years before,
was maimed by the glass
he'd fallen through,

though she believes her mother
who says the cloud is happy
to see them standing
at the top of the stairs.
Decades later, her memory lives

on napkins and envelopes
strewn about the house, and this
story is another particle of dust
caught in the light.

THE GREAT FORGETTING

Lone Mary, collapsible woman—
>					how often do you think of your brother?

>	You carried him on your back for three days before he fell heavy
from your shoulders, laid to rest at the base of a mountain.

>			Is the weight of the living different than that of the murdered?

>	You arrived in a new country with one dress, a pair of shoes,
a dead brother somewhere back in Lebanon.

>					Where is the word I'm looking for?

>	At some point there was a house with a roof where your son
swung a cat by its tail, launching it to the moon or the gutter.

>				Will a language vanish if a child is beaten long enough?

>	In that house he was Yusuf, and later became Joseph,
who he remained until his death. Eventually, he could no longer remember you.

>				How do fathers become moveable objects?

>	My father carried Joseph—his father—westward, across the desert's back.
Our language is that of the pallbearer, the troubled business of carrying.

>			Did you mean for him to drag his children from their hiding places?

>	Joseph forgot your name but took his insulin by muscle memory,
tossed the needle on the counter for someone else to bury.

>					Is this the moon or the gutter?

>	He devoured every sweet thing he could catch in his fist.
His wife found the gun laid out on the bed, delicate as a doll's shoe.

>	The dying man says, *The children kept asking me to kill them, but I couldn't do it.*

In the water, he is starving and alone.
There is only the quiet, and a dollar in his pocket.

        He tried to catch the fish, a flash of silver
that slipped from his hands and escaped downstream.

MARY ANSWERS ALL MY QUESTIONS

It is green where we are headed.
I think of the mountain more.
And the road.
And the river.
I look back.
Do not return there.
Family becomes heavier.
Once they're dead.
Like everything else.
It starts to sink.
The sun rises.
No one listens.
A language vanishes easily.
If a child is beaten long enough.
Fathers forget your name.
How to take their insulin.
He was always angry.
I didn't mean for that to happen.
But.
If a man chooses to starve.
That is his right.
Now he's small.
As his children were.
Dragged by the ankles.
From beneath their beds.
It's quiet.
Now.
I feel my throat.
Like another door.
Behind that.
A memory. Behind that door
a memory.
Here.
There is no need.
For food or names.

GRIEF

In the mail: a brochure for cemetery plots.
Dad and I laugh hard about that.
He knows you can't plan for death
and I know he's going to live forever.

That same week an old friend dies—
there is a gun. A bed. That time of year.
Dad puts this phone call on a shelf with the others,
holds the quiet in the cradle of his arm.

NESTING

v. 1. (of certain wild animals) to make or choose a home. 2. to fit (a set or series of similar things) inside a larger one: a bird hides in the gutters / of my grandmother's house. I wake gasping / from a dream where she is swallowed / by a heaving ocean. / The bird builds a house / out of leaves, / mud, / an old frisbee. / I can never outrun the flood / even in dreams. The bird / settles in. The roof of my grandmother's house / sags downward / into a smile. When I walk / through whatever afterward / is promised, it will be / pinecones and peanut butter, / birdseed and blueberries, / and I will hear her / clear as water.

HOME FOR DINNER

You're trying home on again
and join us around the dinner table.
I keep my distance.

You pull family over your head
like an old sweater.
We cross our fingers in prayer.

Hands shake, legs jitter.
I hear everything you could have been
rattling around inside you.

You are still trapped in the mountains
and your father's pulse still disappears
under your mother's fingertips.

Arizona couldn't save you,
all that dry heat and red earth.

HOME FOR DINNER, REPRISE

Grandma prayed to the right saint
and found her missing rings inside
her mother's empty teapot.

For years the rings hid in the belly
of her secret. She finally told our grandfather,
his mouth a grim line the way it always was

when we wandered too far from the garden.
You found a hole in the fence that had always been there.
You didn't want to come back.

Said you liked the heat—too comfortable
to be a lost thing inside any house
that would take you,

to break bread at any table
where you felt welcome,
at any table with bread.

THE ARCHETYPE

I stop and I look. I listen and I wait. I am
what he makes of me. I do not walk
on water, but sink beneath its mirror
        heavy as a house,
just like a woman; I make a river
what it is, what he longs for
in the early morning, voice dark
with whiskey. I always wake to it.
        I am what he says
I am; a gentle guide
back towards the surface.

ANNA M.

for Anneliese Michel

Patient A, before the convulsions, described "devil faces" and was diagnosed with epileptic psychosis. There are doctors' reports of forgotten time and repeated genuflection. A whole year passed before the seizures stopped. The autopsy revealed malnourishment, dehydration, negligent homicide, and pneumonia. Spiders starved in the temporal lobe.

:::

      How many ways can a body bend
      inside an empty house?

July is a cruel month
to kneel so often the bones shatter.

      Eventually, my face swelled
      where God should be.

Voices hovered behind me,
undulating beneath my left shoulder.

      I tasted copper. Smelled like fire.
      Even the sound of food, the spoons and forks—

I starved on spiders, real and otherwise.
Quickly, I forgot

      the pills: aolept, dilantin, etc.
      Light became too knowable.

I joined in the idolatry,
stuck hands down my throat

      and found nothing. Everyone
      entered the garden

but me. Cleansed sixty-seven times
before I remembered my name.

BAD LUCK POEM

The beach in my head is killing me
and the ocean makes no sense.

The most important moments
in a girl's life are born of indifference

and curiosity; I find a butterfly wing
in a pile of driftwood and hold it

in my palm, which is all I can do.
Butterflies do not have pockets

for iron nails or smooth white stones.
No hats for a father to forget on the bed.

No wolf in her mouth that advises
against complimenting the neighbor's shoes.

I'm unsure what that bright cloud
over the hill means. The therapist says

I am tasked with beginning.
Oh, I say, *so I am burdened with genesis.*

No, she says, you are responsible for your own healing.
Oh, I say, *so I am afflicted with dawn.*

From behind, a hand rests
on my left shoulder, heavy and dark.

ADAM FORCING EVE TO EAT AN APPLE

Françoise Gilot, 1946, pencil and crayon on paper, 20x26"

She clasps the dark, piercing the skin.
Tempt these things that come. Weeping,
eyes open and clear, she was
the type of catastrophe he didn't want
to avoid. Later, she composed the scene:

the bowl of fruit, the green echo.

DREAM CATACLYSM *or* TERMINATOR 2 IS THE BETTER MOVIE

    I. Sarah Connor

"Like being born, maybe."
"Look, the dream's the same."
"Children:" "burnt paper," "not moving."
"The wave hits
        and they fly apart like leaves."
"Not a dream, you moron."
"It's real." "A highway at night."
"It happens."
        [panicked hysterical rage]
"You think you're alive." "But nothing
dead will go." "I know
it happens." "Everything you see,"
"a dream."

    II. T-800, Cyberdyne Systems Model 101

I have some vague understanding
of liquid and metal. I know now
why you cry. You feel better. Clearer.

You found a big truck. A useful tool
for plowing through buildings and men.
You see a girl in your dreams.

Sitting by the ocean. Climbing a tree.
Band-Aids on her knees.
Her back is always turned to you.

You are trying to get to her.
You are running through the trees.
You say, "Don't open the door
to anyone but me."

SUNDOWN

i am telling you i'm outside myself
        in the room behind the door

behind the door the light is on
        & i am home

i promise   i am not lost
        in the grocery   wandering

about my four lemons & a pair of socks
        i gathered you in my basket

with a bushel of keys i need these
        for the plane ride back somewhere

i can't think of   what door
        do i stand behind

it's on the tip of my name the door
        that i stand behind   the box

where my head goes where my dinner
        lives   where children make

potted plants become swing sets
        every library i dream

of the afternoon where we hung
        pinecones from a cheek

& waited for winged mammals
        to turn another branch

my children live inside the telephone
        it never remembers

who i go or where i leave my numbers
        she walked into the citrus & never

turned sideways that's what they'll collect
      about me when i am

on my shelf   behind a door
      deep inside a cupboard

THE NEIGHBOR

screams and takes a bat to the windshield
of a cop car. The cop does not draw
his weapon, merely raises his hands
as if to soothe a violent animal. We don't know
the neighbor's family, but they've come to hide
in our living room. His wife covers her mouth
and the skin on her hand is like tissue paper.
My parents give her a chair to watch his arrest
unfolding through the screen door.
Her children and grandchildren gather
behind her, say *it's okay it's okay*
with their hands on her shoulders.
This has happened before. I was told
not to look, but I peek and see the evening
light expand across their foreheads.
I have biked past that house
for what seems like every afternoon
I've been alive, the eyes
of the Virgin Mary following me
from her station on the lawn.
In the years following, we'd see the old man
seething in his truck in the driveway.
We never saw his family again,
but he'd leave gifts hanging
from plastic bags on our doorknob:
fat green zucchinis and tomatoes
the size of my head that my father would slice
and eat standing in our kitchen.
Mary is still there, fading into the grass, her eyes
and palms fixed upward beyond the tree line.

MYTH MAKER

Fearsome oak rooted in Tuesdays
of black smoke and blue sky
pulled loose like a shoelace.
My father talks in stories,
can stretch a memory for miles.
He had one about hiding a penny
when he was a boy. I don't remember
if it was me or my brother who found it,
but it was there, tucked in a niche
between rocks above our heads.
My father gave the penny to me
for safe keeping. I hid it
in a small ceramic church
with an intricate iron clasp.
Long after I lost the church
my father asked about the penny.
Hearing my confession,
he laughed. *I never hid the penny,*
  he said. *I brought it with me*
and put it there for you to find.
My father, who learned that you can
only outrun the Devil if you want
to live hard enough, gave me magic
in the form of a lie.

THIS DAY

arrange   saltshaker napkin sugarmilk knifespoonfork until perfectly aligned find the angle in everything a hardtrue line between the fact and   the matter it's easier to catch the Eye than to give it she says quickly   now   before   the   boss   comes   home from measuring the ocean or else he'll be lost out west thirty years before the girl finds the hole in   the   ground and   drags   him   out   back to   a   different place   somewhere more   familiar with   water   on   either   side girl   stops   at   a   window   and   climbs down   to a   street   she is looking for someone first   a mother   the   relentless   shake always   a runaway   never   a daughter second our father who art a bastard   hallowed be   thy   grave   every   song   sounds like   a packed   suitcase   doesn't it
      give us   this day

        this day
                and the next

PAST / PRESENT / FUTURE

I. The Sun (Reversed)

Most terrible things happen on Tuesdays,
in my experience. There is always a cherished bowl
that shatters, an unexpected flood, a fire
I did not intend to start, swallowing
the house and everyone in it.

> I am the deer in the trees,
> the deer with the sad eyes.

II. The Star

In every memory, the sun floats full behind her head.

> III. Queen of Wands (Reversed)

On a hot day in August, she reached for me
across a table, tears in her eyes—I swear
she was human then, my human mother,
with wild hair and a secret. Mother,
human, asking: *What are you hiding?*

THINGS WE DO & HAVE ALWAYS DONE

Kitty Genovese, 1935–1964

.

        "the sudden glow" "of bedroom lights"
        "frightened" "one person"
        "called after" "the" "dead"

                                        "people fail"
                                        "at 3:20 A.M."

:

For the migraine: a bowl of water
above the head, a drop of oil

and if it takes a certain shape
the girl is cursed.

Urge her away from places
with too many trees, harsh interruptions

in the landscape of fingers, arms,
nape of the neck.

They say those boys will plant
a foreign object in a loose cigarette

and wait for the slow-yellow
light to close the dark.

What can be done for a girl
who's caught the Eye?

I am a vessel for things my mother has seen
but won't speak, though she spits

at the sound of a word.
Rub the membrane of an egg

against the girl's skull.
The yolk will pull

the mold from her blood
and hold it.

∴

    "tree-lined" "Kitty"
    "in" "her red Fiat"
      "day after day"
          "She turned off the lights"

    "At night the quiet" "slumbering darkness"
    "halted."

::

My mother witnessed the murder of a stranger
and removed what's precious from sight.

In my eleventh hour
I might've cried out

but some sounds are too familiar
to be effective.

There is safety in a dark bar,
a lover's sweaty hand.

There are things we do
and have always done.

For the hysteric: encase her
in smoke, olive leaves, and salt.

For the wound: a nip of blackberry
brandy from the linen closet.

For what lives in the throat:
soothe with apples.

For the fear: do not exit through the door
you entered.

For the ache: light a candle
and pass the flame

over the girl's stomach.
Watch the shadows dance.

Above her navel, trap
a silver coin in an upturned glass.

She will still appear in stairwells
and parallelograms of sun.

I've been sick
with worry for things I haven't seen.

For the worry: kneel
and light a candle.

I've felt it snag on my teeth
growing backwards, alive inside me.

I've cradled a small flame in my palms
while the mourners wait to burn

through the dark. The lost
can reveal themselves.

I cannot exit through the door
I entered.

∴

        "Lights went on"   "Windows slid open"
        "Lights went out."

"3:35 A.M."

"Miss Genovese"
"Freshly painted"

"held"
          "the"
                    "door"

:::

When I was small, I imagined shadows
watching from the corners of my room.

I hid beneath the covers
knowing if I couldn't see them

they couldn't see me
and therefore weren't real.

Imagining you
that day on the street

you say nothing, see the thing
and hold it.

I'm sorry I didn't follow
but you should know
you'd never catch me
alive in a white dress.

Light cracks the shell,
love identifies the body.

I write notes
and pin them to the front door.

I have secrets named Mary and Dee.
I have a stomachache.

I remember your cool hand
on my cheek.

I've congealed into an uncertain shape,
but what can be done?

He found me, mama,
then kept finding me.

Please. Come
to the window.

::..

        "he saw her"
        "3:50 A.M."
        "how simple"

        "A phone call,"
        "a lovers quarrel."

                        "Frankly, we were afraid."

        "A distraught woman, wiping her hands"
            "went" "to" "the window"
        "the light"   "made it difficult to see"

::::

I found myself
in the arms of a woman

I didn't know but knew
her fear, saw it

alive at the center
of her forehead.

She was so sorry
and so afraid.

:::::.

        "open" "the door"

        "4:25 A.M."

                "take the body"

:::::

Then,
the people came out.

III.

*Come back! Even as a shadow,
even as a dream.*

Euripides

BIRTH OF VENUS

Sandro Botticelli, ~1486, tempura painting, 5' 8" x 9' 2"

Memory is a human promise I do not see
        the line where my life lives
                I woke fully formed inside

a collection of yellow dresses
        ducks on a string
                peaches in a jar

preserving sweetness for the crumbling
        house What makes me sigh
                & become a woman

waiting in a window as slices of fruit
        turn bruised on a white plate
                I am careful with my totems

the saints hanging
        in a mirror We are waiting for something
                to happen I lose the shape

for a time The line
        manifests in corners
                shuffles through a crack

to stretch inside a square of light
        soft belly raised
                to a trembling hand

DURING A CHAT SESSION, THE THERAPIST DISCOURAGES ME FROM ASTRAL PROJECTION

[07:36 PM]

    i suggest a zen space in the home
    possibly next to a garden window if you have it

[07:38 PM]

    i know it seems silly but it will show
    at least you can control something

[07:40 PM]

    IDK who youre hoping to see or what youre hoping to hear
    but I know you prefer direct communication

[07:41 PM]

    as opposed to indentations on the bed
    or the dream of the door opening

                                                  Your therapist is typing...

[07:44 PM]

    how you were yanked upward by your left arm & spun toward the window
    where the feral cats scream only to find the door closed
    & slats of light resting on the bedroom floor

[07:45 PM]

    there was no one behind you

                                                  Your therapist is typing...

[07:47 PM]

    maybe youre hoping this will give you a way to write about the sand dollars
    that appeared on the beach one winter

[07:48 PM]

    how did u describe it?

[07:48 PM]

    like the moon had shattered

[07:50 PM]

    i know your arm is numb. I dont mean 2 minimize the situation

[07:52 PM]

    maybe the voice you heard was your own as you explained to your mother
    the feeling that sat like a rock in your stomach
    while someone you love died far away

Your therapist is typing…
Your therapist is typing…
Your therapist is typing…

A GUIDE FOR MOVING THROUGH

I.

Hear the television first, the volume
crashing through the kitchen, the hallway,
to greet you like a dog at the front door.

Follow the voice of the news anchor
and find the old woman surrounded
by envelopes, bills, receipts, napkins,
(some used) organized into piles
her children misunderstand.

A life filed into boxes.
Hills she cannot get around.
She pries the tape from cardboard cracks
and roots through what she can't remember.

Dish towels. Anniversary cards.
Photographs that once spilled down the walls.
China dolls. Tea sets. If she can't see them
they must not be there, or never were.

Ask if she's gotten rid of anything.
If she's cleaned. Stop asking
when she starts to panic.

Watch her salvage a birthday sign
held together by glue and staples.
Let her hide it in a drawer. Forget
you saw anything.

II.

The last time you stood in the doorway
was the last time.

A new family will walk through it
when you are gone.

Months later, drive past
in its new color.

MYTHOLOGY

You think I'd let this girl
parade around my house like it's hers,
take my children, leave me
       with nothing?
I stepped down from fire and light
into picket fences and apple pie
like I wasn't stolen, like you didn't
pluck me from gods,
       out of rock and stone.
There are worse things than a dress
laced with poison. A crown. I heard
she started foaming at the mouth,
that her blood curdled, and she fell
       like a castle wall.
I wanted to be human for you—
wear my hair the way you like,
raise your children, win your battles,
       quietly.
You wanted to make a fool of me.
Rather I be drowned than vengeful,
prove that a river is only a river
when there's a woman to sink
       to the bottom.
Years from now they'll wonder
about our love story. In the beginning
you liked my magic so much
       you took it. I let you
lure me down that mountain.
The Chorus spits the word
murderer at my feet, forgetting
I am royalty. Forgetting
       I am mother,
but don't they always
confuse a loving mother
       with a woman scorned.
You killed our children
before I ever touched them.

What was I supposed to do?
Have you ever known a mother's touch
to be anything but warm—a blanket
of lambswool, a chariot suspended
       by the light of the sun.

HEAVY

The world is heavy and full
of accidents
                    Like sand
                    through a screen
                                      A storm door
                                      clanging shut

You stole
the plums
                    I did nothing
                    to stop you
                                      I should know
                                      when to beg

Love shouldn't give
bruised knees
                    Someone had
                    to drag the body
                                      From the river
                                    I suppose

I thought
I was the body
                    I stare at the drain
                    and wait
                                      The fish
                                    came

and cleaned
my bones
                    I think
                    I'm the river
                                    The mud
                                    the fish

In the heron's mouth
its yellow eye
                    You are not
                    the fisherman
                                    The body
                                    he became

Not the rock
he slipped on

                    Or the wife waiting
                    for anything alive

                                        To start swimming
                                        from the reeds

But the hook
its grin

I FEEL LIKE A GIRL

        I don't feel like a girl
all the time more than anything I feel lonely
        I feel like a girl around other women
especially if they're all talking at once
        gathered around a pot of boiling water
a boy walks me to the corner and points me home
        I feel so much like a girl
and not an amorphous shadow
        I wish I'd been a teengirl
in the traditional sense I long
        for the quiet mania of a first kiss
a first rebellion a window
        enough to the ground
I feel like an actor a parakeet
        I feel like maybe
I'm scared to be a girl
        or I feel like a girl when I'm scared
I feel like a girl when I eat
        sugar and when I cry
I feel like a girl when I gossip
        when I sit crooked when I know
something I feel like a girl
        when I blush and when I lie
and when no one listens
        to me or when I lose my
train of thought on the street
        an older man tells me I'm beautiful
and mom asks why are you so bothered
        I feel like a girl when I cry
but I said that already
        mostly I feel ghostly
phantasmic and afraid I feel most
        like a girl in the dark

ODE TO A HOME WAXING KIT

In the wet heat of my fourteenth summer
I walk toward the pharmacy. Timid, I wander
the aisles and pluck a kit off the shelf.
Shiny pink women promise me
        easy and painless.
Lady at the register doesn't look up,
but raises her eyebrows at my crumpled money,
purses her pink painted lips at my sweaty palms.
I walk home, plastic bag swinging from my fingers
heavy as a hunted boar. The sun heaves a sigh
and settles in the neighbor's yard.
I let the shower run, face myself, peel
the paper off the sticky side of one wax strip,
press it on my upper lip. I can't know
this will end in tears—raw, painful pink.
Pink like a slap. Pink like failure,
        but I'm no coward.
Pain lets you know you're alive.
I want to be alive. I have to be here.
I have to do this. I can't wait
to be hairless and rose-colored.
        Later, I wrap my shame in the dead
animal it came in, shove it in the garbage,
receipt and all.

AT THE HOSPITAL, AGAIN

Grandma and I take the same white pill.

Would you remind me why I'm here? she asks.
        You went missing, I tell her. You forgot the way home.

Be careful out there, she says. *So many ways to get lost.*
        How terrifying the world became while I was away.

My mother is elbow deep in earth when she gets the call,
        caked in worms and mud. Her siblings say it falls on her

to save the bird. Their mother's parakeet, alone in her house,
the house with the cuckoo clocks, the tablecloths,

the daily medication disintegrating under the couch.
        She's your mother, too, my mother starts, but the line cuts.

Mosquitos eat her calves and I swallow my pill.

I walk across a field and wake up in the hospital.
        I am among friends.

Electrical pathways grow like weeds through a ventricle,
        a surgeon pokes a wire in my heart and deems it lazy but normal.

        Wasted a perfectly good Thursday.

Grandma hits the ground like a joyous hand slapping a knee.
        Another accident. I dream of the animal

exploded by a semi. I am comfortable with death but the sight of this
        unbearable mass makes me vomit in a bush.

The bird died anyway. We take our pills.

A red gash forms along her hairline. This is not the place
        I expected. My mother's face

emerges from storm clouds, enormous and crying,
	as she shakes me awake. I don't remember when

   and how I got here.

CHERYL CRANE REMEMBERS THE FLOWERS

The day they started coming
   my mother tried so hard to hide them,

but soon roses overwhelmed the kitchen,
   rotting in the sink, drifting through the living room

toward the closed bedroom door.
   Mother said there was a noise

in his throat. I don't even remember
him walking into the knife.

As far as I know,
   he and I, we came together

and we parted. I remember
   the smell, the light

beneath the door,
   her punctured hands

bleeding. The holes
   were small enough

at first. She would cut the stems
   and watch the water

swirl around the drain,
   turn from red to pink to clear.

Just thorns, she said.
   Doing what thorns do.

ME & MOM & LITTLE GIRL BLUE

      At the dollar store I pick a bouquet
of pinwheels. A familiar voice crackles from the car
radio singing *come on come on* and I don't ask
about the beer in the backseat or the unassuming
pumpkin. I know the gifts change. Sometimes,
maybe, chrysanthemums, sometimes
a particularly interesting rock, sometimes nothing
because I'm not always there when she is.
      There is something about a churchyard in autumn,
how the afternoon catches on what was meant to be
temporary, a name etched in iron, fading into the mud.
      She doesn't believe in ghosts or aliens or anything
that only claims to be true, but she does believe in the sun
and the butterflies she grows in my old bedroom
that hang around the yard for days after their release.
      Most of all, she believes in the blues
and the lonely people it belongs to, who translate
grief into magic, a grave into a birthday party.
      My mother's as good as a poet—she says things
like *Everyone wants to feel beautiful* or *Everyone wants
to find a pattern* though most fade into one color.
      I've seen winter grab her wrist too hard,
bruises blooming where it's touched her. I want to kill it
for every room in our house turned dark
and unforgiving. Begging's not the same as wanting
something so bad you have to cry—soon enough, a girl
gets so lonely she becomes another friend found
in a motel room, through no fault of her own
but a longing for color.
      At the church, we lift our offerings from the car,
arrange the pumpkin, the beer, the pinwheels and watch them
spin in place of a headstone. Janis says we only gotta do one thing well
and everything she says sounds like a promise.
      Everything she tells me I believe.

PAST / PRESENT / FUTURE

      I. The Queen of Pentacles

A collection of empty plates
is called a forgetting.
Don't ask me if or why I haven't eaten.
I couldn't tell you. My neck swung open
and everything that poured out was a lie.

      II. Ace of Swords (Reversed)

Paranoid about the spiders in my shirt,
I think of spaceships and planets,
the way trees are only shadows
depending on the light and my mother's voice
saying, *We have always been like this.*

      III. Four of Wands (Reversed)

I don't recognize the flushed animal
in the mirror. She looks too much
like a painting. That's her on the roof
and in the kitchen—within her
I will find flowers and a spine.

I STAND GRIPPING THE BRIDGE

ugly and powerful,
rain-lashed in the Arctic turmoil.

A crow—ancient
paraphernalia—clings high:

*You cannot make more
than the sea can replace.*

This is fine, but ruthless.
Below me, a dozen whales breach

in an empty berth, bored girls
swimming free.

I want to ride them
—blue shadows pursued

by ocean-going men,
a lifetime harpooned.

VIGNETTES FROM THE END

I.

  There was that winter, like every winter
before or after, where the bay froze
into a steamed mirror and the boys
came upon a place that held them, determined
they could walk all the way to Kismet.
  Brave expeditioners, coats zipped up to the eyes,
they pressed on until they could see the lighthouse
then turned back, not because they were scared
or because the ice had become soft (which it hadn't)
but because the sun had set. Around the corner,
their mothers chopped garlic
  and fried meat, unaware.

II.

  I learn to navigate waves before
I know how to swim.
A mouthful of sand is a birthright.
This is a test: can you recognize
a riptide from the shore. Can you spot
beach glass in a collage of muscle,
horseshoe crab, driftwood.
  Do you remember that winter
the sand dollars appeared. Thousands
of tiny corpses stretched before us
like the moon had shattered
  into a beaded curtain.

III.

  My mother rips down Ocean Parkway,
lays on her horn when the car ahead pulls over
to feed the deer. *That's how they get hit*, she says, furious.
  That's how the babies die. She tells me
about a feral cat that circles the deli parking lot

and calls for her kittens. One was found
in the tailpipe of a pickup truck, the other two
still missing. The owner leaves a dish of milk by the door.
I say, *You're not supposed to give cats milk.*
That's not the point, she says.
It's that she kept looking
        and I wanted to cry.

IV.

      You can visit the highest peak
where a poet wrote about vast grassland,
its unending stretch from here
to Montauk, now so forested all you can see
is the county water tower at the base of a hill.
Drive five minutes and there's a mall with
      I contain multitudes
inscribed on the wall outside of Macy's
and yet we mourn a fallen tree.
      What a waste, we say,
a living thing yanked from the root.

V.

      It is difficult for me to talk
about butterflies. A pair of them circle me—
a you-and-I swirling in a wind
they do not understand, travelling in warped lines
      down an empty, frigid beach.

VI.

      Here, where any mother can wither you
with a look, the snap of her gum, the tilt of her head,
I learned that we all have a bit of meanness in us.
      It just depends on how you use it.
The women at the salon say *oh honey,*
cluck at my split ends, nails bitten
down to the root. They ask about school,

if I have a boyfriend or a job, remind me
        the beginning is all I know for sure.

VII.

        Three warm bodies travel
through the dunes, emerge on a strange
and familiar planet, the moon's light
dust against their outlines, simple as salt
and water. They incantate within
the impossible roar. Every seven seconds
        the lighthouse
chases them up the beach.
Followed by the watchful deer,
they run toward the parking lot
where they speed away like thieves,
        shoes full of sand, mouths open wide.

VIII.

        Yes,
The End is really
the end. I promise
there is only ocean
        and nothing else.

ODE TO A SCENE IN *MOONSTRUCK*

I could watch Olympia Dukakis make eggs-in-a-hole
for the rest of my life. Just that one scene on loop:
the closeup of the buttered cast iron, the slices
of good bread (and you know it's *good* bread),
the yolk, bright and wiggling in its basket
and, finally, the peppers, greasy gems
effortlessly flipped. In that moment I swear
Olympia Dukakis is my mother, is any woman
in my family (and yes, maybe that makes me Cher)
sliding a precious object onto my plate, lamenting
about the house, *We'll sell the house
because grandma's dead and everybody's left me,*
even though I'm sitting right here, ma.
Olympia Dukakis isn't worried about the moon
or its size or what brings one person into the arms
of another, as if a rock floating in the sky has any say
in how she wastes her time. No, she is preoccupied
with more pressing matters like, again, the house,
breakfast right now, dinner tonight, the bruise
on her daughter's neck. She doesn't care
about the inevitability of love (she is well aware)
or about little boys and their obsessions
with what doesn't belong to them.
One day that stupid rock could come
hurtling toward her kitchen, which has stood
for a hundred years, and she would still raise
one crooked finger to the man standing closest and say,
*No matter what you do, you're gonna die
just like everybody else.*

WHEN THE STORY ENDS

We can't see green at night
you say. Something about the moon

and its language. A fire appears
in your hands. You tell me

a story about cresting a mountain.
In the vast expanse of trees, you made

out mounds of emberlight
dotting the countryside,

each the bloody center
of a coal. You thought

it was a celebration, maybe.
When the guide told you

it was only people burning
their trash, you couldn't help

but laugh. I laugh too
when the story ends. Somewhere

a two-headed trout is aching
to be unwatered. That night

you heard the monolith's slow hum
hover above us. I hadn't

told you about this forest's
reputation for green

lights floating in the sky. I dream
I paint myself a particular color

and appear to you among the flickering
piles of garbage.

I like to think
you'd see me.

NOTES

"In the Glasshouse" is written for Susanne Ussing's sculpture titled "In the Greenhouse."

"Ode to Crazy Girls" references the Phoebe Bridgers song "This is the End."

"I Help Lara Croft with Her First Kill" references the 2013 video game *Tomb Raider*, played all the way through by the author at least eight times.

"Words Underlined in a Used Copy of The Collected Poems of Sylvia Plath" takes lines from Harper Perennial's 1992 edition of *The Collected Poems of Sylvia Plath*, edited by Ted Hughes.

"Putting on Emily Dickinson's Clothes" is written after the sam sax and Billy Collins poems of the same name.

The first part of "Dream Cataclysm *or* Terminator 2 Is the Better Movie" is comprised of lines from Sarah Connor's opening monologue in *Terminator 2: Judgement Day* (1991), performed by Linda Hamilton.

The title for the poem "Things We Do & Have Always Done" comes from the term *benedicaria* or *way of blessing*, a newish term for some loosely related family-based folk traditions, particularly in southern Italy and Sicily. These practices (many of which are described in the poem) have also been called folk magic or witchcraft but, historically, there is no word for *benedicaria*. It is simply called *the things we do and have always done*.

All quoted sections from "Things We Do & Have Always Done" are erasures from a 1964 *New York Times* article called "Thirty-Eight Who Saw Murder Didn't Call the Police."

"Mythology" is inspired by Euripides' tragedy, *Medea*.

"Cheryl Crane Remembers the Flowers" is based on Cheryl Crane, the daughter of actor Lana Turner, who stabbed her mother's lover to death at the age of 14 during a domestic struggle.

"Me & Mom & Little Girl Blue" uses lines from the Janis Joplin song, "Cry Baby."

ACKNOWLEDGEMENTS

Great thanks to the editors and readers of the following publications, where some of these poems first appeared.

Apricity Press: "Grief"
Chronogram: "Nesting"
Blue Mountain Review: "The Great Forgetting"
Empty House Press: "The Tower" (as "Saturday")
Half Mystic: "Me & Mom & Little Girl Blue"
Ocean State Review: "At the Hospital, Again," "Ode to a Scene in Moonstruck"
Palette Poetry: "Lost Things"
RHINO Poetry: "I Help Lara Croft With Her First Kill"
Rumble Fish Quarterly: "Anna M."
Tinderbox Poetry Journal: "In the Glasshouse"
Poetry by Chance (anthology): "Birth of Venus"
Bodega Magazine: "Dream Cataclysm," "Sundown"

—

Thank you to my parents, Joe and Suzin Zogbi, who have cultivated my creative side since I first picked up a pen, for teaching me how to lead with love, to suffer no fools, and most importantly, how to tell a story. To my little brother, Joey, for keeping me humble. And thank you to the rest of my large and loud family, past and present, who inspired many of these poems.

To my grandmothers: Rose Marie Zogbi, a shining example of quiet strength. And Rosemary Mango, for the book of fairy tales, for your faith in me, and for waiting.

To my favorite teachers: Kevin Dineen, who taught me about perspective and reading out loud; Pauline Uchmanowicz who, on the first day we met, asked me, "What are you tending towards?" A large portion of this book is an attempt to answer that question.

Thank you to: Mark Bibbins, Elaine Equi, Camille Rankine, Robert Polito, and all my professors and friends at The New School, all of whom helped shape the poems in this book to what they are now. Thank you for reading, for challenging, for listening, etc. Treehouse forever.

To Jared Singer, Julie Zuckerman and everyone who knew me in my slam poetry days. Some of these poems you saw in their earliest and most vulnerable stages. Thank you for your guidance.

To Victoria D'Esposito, for the beautiful cover and for understanding my vision. To Pete Perry, for taking the pictures. To Nicole Follini, my career advisor, my team captain, my day one, my sister in all things. To Bekah Hack, for everything. Seriously, for everything. LYLAS.

Thank you to the fine people at Finishing Line Press and my editor Christen Kincaid, for seeing the potential in my little book.

Finally, thank you to all the women in my life who have guided me, pushed me, listened to me, fed me, held me, cried with me, and on and on to the ends of the earth—this book is for you.

Emily Zogbi is a writer, editor, and poet from Long Island. In 2021, she earned her MFA in poetry from The New School. Her work has been published in *Chronogram, Rumble Fish Quarterly, Tinderbox Poetry Journal, RHINO Poetry, Half Mystic,* and *Ocean State Review*, among others. Zogbi was the recipient of the 2021 Sappho Poetry Prize from Palette Poetry. She has worked in book publishing, entertainment journalism, childcare, and unemployment, but she mostly enjoys estate sales, bad movies, and collecting rocks. She wishes she had been a dancer.

www.ingramcontent.com/pod-product-compliance
Lightning Source LLC
Chambersburg PA
CBHW020337170426
43200CB00006B/420